Book of Grievances

Book of Grievances

Published by Amazon

SINGLETON, TIARA ILEISHA, Author
Book of Grievances

Printed in the United States of America.

This book presents the grievance submitted by the author to the judicial board, together with relevant public docket records. It is provided solely for informational and archival purposes. This content reflects the author's submission and official public records and is not a legal judgment or statement by the court. This content does not constitute a legal ruling, opinion, or advice. Readers are encouraged to interpret the material in its factual context. Readers should not interpret this as legal advice. All references to the judge's name in the grievance have been replaced with "the Judge" for privacy and safety. All references to the defense attorney's name have been replaced with "the defense attorney" or "the defendant's private attorney" for privacy and safety.

Note: All references to the judge's name in the grievance have been replaced with "the judge" for privacy and safety. All references to the defense attorney's name have been replaced with "the defense attorney" or "the defendant's private attorney" for privacy and safety.

Original Grievance

Submission to the Judicial Conduct Board

To: Judicial Conduct Board of Pennsylvania

Date: January 16, 2026

Re: Grievance Regarding The Judge — Sentencing Hearing, CP-51-CR-0007801-2023

Dear Board Members,

Please find enclosed my formal grievance regarding the conduct of the Judge during the sentencing hearing in my rape case. The arrest date was October 20, 2023. The guilty verdict was rendered on August 8, 2025, and the sentencing hearing took place on January 16, 2026. This grievance is submitted in accordance with the Judicial Conduct Board procedures.

The purpose of this submission is to formally bring to the Board's attention specific conduct by the Judge during the sentencing proceeding that I believe warrants review under the applicable judicial conduct standards. Enclosed is a detailed account of statements, behaviors, and decisions during the sentencing proceeding that I experienced as prejudicial, minimizing, and psychologically corrosive, including unaddressed actions by the defendant's family.

I provide this information in good faith, with respect for the judicial process, and with the goal of highlighting the impact such conduct had on me as the victim, as well as the potential risks to other survivors and the integrity of the judicial process. I am prepared to provide any additional information or documentation if required.

Thank you for your careful attention and consideration.

Respectfully Submitted,

Tiara Ileisha Singleton

Statement of Concern

I am submitting this grievance to document the unprofessional conduct and apparent bias in favor of the defendant that occurred during the sentencing hearing in my rape case today, and the impact it had on me as the victim.

During the sentencing hearing, the Judge made multiple unprofessional statements and engaged in unjust behavior that I experienced as prejudicial, minimizing, and re-traumatizing; especially in the context of a rape conviction.

Specific Conduct Observed

1. Defendant's Attorney on Victim's Side

   During the sentencing hearing, the defendant's attorney was seated on the victim's side of the courtroom. This placement was highly inappropriate and contributed to the sense of intimidation and imbalance I experienced as the victim, compounding the retraumatization caused by the proceeding.

2. Victim Displacement

   The defendant and his family received more empathy and respect than I did as the victim. The defendant's family was allowed to speak before I, the victim, had the opportunity to address the court. My family was not invited or permitted to address the court at any point during the sentencing hearing.

   During this portion of the proceeding, the defendant's private attorney, characterized the defendant as having "the privilege" of a better upbringing, more "family support," and superior schooling, while implying that I did not share these advantages, stating that at least "my" client "knows what it is like" to be raised in a family. This statement directly contrasted the defendant's upbringing with mine and reinforced bias against me as the victim. The defense attorney then offered the floor to any family member who wished to speak.

Following this, members of the defendant's family, including his grandparents, addressed the court, pleading for leniency and emphasizing the defendant's religious upbringing. My family, by contrast, was not permitted to speak.

During the sentencing proceeding, while the court was actively in session, members of the defendant's family made audible remarks from the gallery. At one point, a member of the defendant's family stated words to the effect of, "I'm going to kill her." I cannot state with certainty whether this statement was directed toward me or toward the District Attorney; however, because it was made audibly during the proceeding and in the context of prior intimidation, the remark was alarming and escalated my fear for safety.

Additionally, while the proceeding was ongoing, members of the defendant's family made comments suggesting that the defendant would "only do three months" and would then be released. These statements reflected a dismissive and unserious attitude toward the rape conviction and further reinforced the perception that the severity of the crime and its impact were being minimized within the courtroom environment. No corrective action or admonishment was issued by the court in response to these statements.

These remarks, and the court's allowance of them, shifted focus away from the defendant's criminal conduct, reinforced victim displacement, and contributed significantly to the retraumatization I experienced during the sentencing hearing.

This pattern of victim displacement was not isolated to sentencing, but was consistent with prior proceedings in this case. During earlier testimony before the Judge, the defendant's private attorney engaged in sexually explicit questioning toward me as the victim, screaming a series of questions. Demanding that I answer (his questions) if I was watching or staring at the defendant's penis swing through his "ballshorts" at the time of the assault. I do not recall the defense attorney's exact phrasing, but the substance and repetition of the questioning were degrading, humiliating, and irrelevant to any legitimate issue before the court. When this line of questioning caused me visible distress on the stand, the Judge did not intervene to limit or redirect the questioning. Instead, I was admonished for my emotional reaction and language, and the court stated, in substance, that while this may be new to me, the defense attorney was permitted to ask such questions. This response reinforced the displacement of the victim and conveyed judicial tolerance of sexually demeaning questioning directed at a rape survivor.

Notably, the (defense) attorney engaging in this conduct has received a public reprimand from the Disciplinary Board of the Supreme Court of Pennsylvania (2020), reflecting prior findings of professional misconduct. While I raise this solely as contextual background, the court's allowance of this line of questioning—particularly given that history—further contributed to my sense of imbalance, intimidation, and retraumatization throughout these proceedings.

After I was finally given the opportunity to address the court to read my victim impact statement, the Judge made jokes, laughed, and commented in ways that were deeply harmful, abhorrent, and inappropriate. Her misconduct and tone were extremely distressing and further contributed to the imbalance, intensifying my experience of displacement as the victim. I felt physically unable to remain in the courtroom and had to exit before hearing the defendant's sentence. Immediately outside the courtroom, I fell to my knees, overwhelmed by the emotional distress caused by the proceeding.

Throughout the course of this case, the defendant was allowed by the Judge's court to postpone the trial more than three times. The sentencing date was also delayed, bringing this case into its third holiday period since it was first docketed. At all times, I was fully prepared to proceed with the trial and sentencing and never requested any postponement. In stark contrast, repeated delays were granted to the defendant, prolonging the proceedings and significantly heightening the emotional distress and revictimization I experienced. This further reinforced the imbalance, victim displacement, and lack of consideration for my well-being.

Additionally, the repeated postponements resulted in the trial proceeding on the two-year anniversary of the rape itself. Jury selection was scheduled to begin on August 4, 2025, with my testimony scheduled for August 5, the anniversary of the assault. Despite this, the defense attorney was permitted to extend jury selection into August 6, further delaying my testimony. I was required to wait in the courthouse from early morning until mid-afternoon on the anniversary of the assault before proceedings began. No acknowledgment, accommodation, or consideration was offered regarding the significance of this date or the foreseeable emotional harm caused. Allowing the trial and testimony to proceed in this manner further demonstrated the displacement of the victim and the court's failure to exercise trauma-informed discretion.

3. Complimentary remarks toward the Defendant

   The Judge made multiple complimentary statements about the defendant, highlighting his spirituality and education. In stark contrast; she stated from the bench that I (the victim of the crime) will have my whole life ahead of me and "will get over it." The Judge also announced to the court that the defendant had attended "Lincoln University." This public emphasis on the defendant's accomplishments and character, juxtaposed with the minimization of my trauma, further reinforced the imbalance and bias I experienced during the sentencing hearing.

4. Victim-blaming Language

   The Judge stated that I, as the victim, "made a bad decision," along with the defendant, that led to the events before the court. "Two people made a bad decision."

5. Minimization of harm

   The Judge stated that I have my whole life ahead of me and that I will "get over it."

6. Inaccurate and harmful characterization of the rape as a "party time"

   During the sentencing hearing, The Judge stated several times that alcohol and drugs were involved and repeatedly referred to the rape as a "party time." This characterization was egregious, factually incorrect and profoundly harmful.

Alcohol was not involved in this case. The police report reflects that only marijuana was reported with the crime. Stating that alcohol and drugs were involved and using this inaccurate statement to explain how "cloudy" the events and judgment may have been; implied impaired memory, shifted responsibility of the defendant at sentencing, and trivialized the seriousness of the offense.

Beyond being inaccurate, referring to a rape as a "party time" inherently implies that the encounter was social, mutual, or enjoyable. This language is extremely dangerous for survivors. The Judge implicitly suggested consent, enjoyment, or shared responsibility, and reframed this violent crime as a casual or recreational event.

Characterizing a rape in this manner trivializes the offense, undermines the seriousness of a rape conviction, and displaces responsibility away from the defendant. As the victim, I experienced this language as deeply insufferable and as an implicit suggestion that the assault was consensual or that I "had fun," which is categorically false.

7. Statements suggesting moral equivalence or negotiation

   Although the Judge acknowledged receiving "excellent" letters from both sides (six were submitted on my behalf), she highlighted the defendant's letters while stating she could not address remaining (victim) letters. This reinforced that the defendant's experience and character were prioritized over the impact of the crime he committed, contributing to the retraumatization I experienced.

   Throughout the sentencing, The Judge also repeatedly stated that she understood "both sides." From the bench, she expressed her uncertainty about how to proceed with sentencing. She also stated that she was "trying to be fair to both sides" while appearing to openly negotiate the sentence with the defendant and his family. This framing suggested a moral equivalence between the victim and the convicted offender, rather than prioritizing accountability and justice. The Judge comments and tone reinforced the displacement of the victim, minimized the severity of this rape conviction, and contributed to the anguish and retraumatization I experienced during the proceeding. It also reinforced that responsibility and harm were being balanced and shared between both the victim and defendant.

The Judge further stated from the bench that the defendant does "not deserve" a longer sentence or to be incarcerated upstate. This statement reflected a personal moral judgment in favor of the defendant rather than an impartial evaluation grounded in the seriousness of the offense, the jury's verdict, or the documented harm caused. In the context of a rape conviction, declaring that a convicted offender does "not deserve" a longer sentence reinforced the minimization of the crime and further demonstrated advocacy and bias toward the defendant.

Ultimately, the Judge sentenced the defendant to 11½–23 months of confinement and up to 3 years probation, far below the standard range for this offense. This sentence starkly contrasts with the severity of the crime. The leniency and the manner in which it was delivered further demonstrate the imbalance in how the proceedings treated the defendant's interests compared with mine as the victim. Unlike the defendant, I never requested delays or postponements and was fully prepared to proceed, emphasizing the stark contrast in diligence and fairness. The sentencing reinforced the sense that my trauma was minimized and that responsibility was being unfairly shifted onto me as the victim.

8. Courtroom demeanor

   The Judge made jokes and laughed during the sentencing hearing, including making an inappropriate, seemingly celebratory remark to the defendant. Exuberantly stating to the defendant from the bench, "Ooooh, you went out with a bang, young man" accompanied by a smirk. In the context of a rape conviction, this phrase carries an active and highly inappropriate sexual connotation. The comment romanticized and trivialized the gravity of the offense. The judge's tone and apparent enthusiasm amplified the effect, contributing directly to the severe psychological corrosion and re-traumatization I experienced as the victim.

9. Statements minimizing risk to the community

   During sentencing, the Judge endorsed and restated the defendant's previous statement to the court that he is "not a danger to the community." The judge also stated from the bench that she doubts the defendant will "put himself in this situation again."

   Despite these statements from the Judge, In the days and weeks prior to the defendant's arrest, the defendant's employer and associates legally threatened me with lawsuits .

   Further harassment included: monitoring/commenting on my social media, messaging me, demanding to meet; and slandering my reputation, sexual orientation and business online. The Internal Affairs Bureau became involved after the defendant's associates cited an Officer's name (Detective from Special Victim's Unit) as a source to confirm slanderous statements, to publicly discredit and intimidate me from pursuing charges. This demonstrates the coordinated and dangerous nature of the harassment.

The defendant's family and defendant continued to engage in repeated intimidation for the duration of this entire case. A member of his family followed me out of the courtroom the day of the preliminary hearing, requiring intervention from my mother. There were also intimidation attempts during separate proceedings in family court; appearances related to the sexual violence restraining order I filed. The day the guilty verdict was read, members of the defendant's family had to be removed from the courtroom due to disruptive behavior. The defendant personally sent notification to my accounts to notify me that he was monitoring my activity.

Violations of The Court's stay-away order (and the PSVI Sexual Violence restraining order) were reported but consistently dismissed. When reporting these incidents to the District Attorney's Office, I was informed that the defendant's conduct was deemed 'not serious enough' to be considered or addressed by the Judge's court. This dismissal of ongoing threats and intimidation directly contradicted the judge's public statements that minimized the defendant's risk. It also reinforces that my safety was not taken seriously.

Even when the defendant was served with the PSVI Restraining Order (11/08/2023); I was further informed by the officer who served it that, upon receipt, the defendant tore up the restraining order as well as the accompanying signature affidavit. As a result, the officer was required to complete a separate document to confirm service. This conduct was not addressed by the court and further contradicts the court's characterization of the defendant as "not a danger to the community."

Additionally, after the defendant was released on bail (11/09/2023) and placed on court supervision (house arrest); I encountered him in public (06/09/2024) at a festival I was attending. I later learned that his presence was permitted by the Judge's court under the characterization of "work." Regardless of that authorization, encountering the defendant in a public setting caused immediate fear and forced me to leave for my safety. This incident further demonstrated the disconnect between the court's repeated minimization of the defendant's risk and the real, destabilizing impact of those decisions on my safety and well-being as the victim.

The accumulation of all these incidents required me to relocate for my safety and resulted in several police reports. Despite this documented history of harassment, the Judge's court continued to minimize the defendant's risk, stating at sentencing that he was "not a danger to the community," ignoring the real and immediate threats I faced.

Ongoing harassment during sentencing

Even during sentencing, the defendant, his family and/or his counsel raised complaints regarding my published books and personal writing on my platforms, despite existing stay-away orders and my lack of any contact with him.

I do not clearly recall the judge's precise phrasing ; just acknowledging that I am still the victim. There was no inquiry, admonishment, or protective consideration directed toward the defendant's continued monitoring of my online activity, its relevance to existing stay-away/restraining orders, or the implications for my safety and risk to the community.

Together, these incidents demonstrate a persistent pattern of the court minimizing the defendant's risk, disregarding documented threats to my safety, and failing to enforce protective orders. The defendant's continued harassment, combined with the lack of judicial accountability, placed me in ongoing, foreseeable danger and highlights a systemic failure to protect me as a victim. The court's inaction not only undermined my safety but also signals to survivors and the public that threats and intimidation may be dismissed or tolerated, exacerbating trauma and eroding trust in the justice system.

Witnessed Reactions

As I was leaving the courtroom—before the defendant's sentence was announced—the impact of the Judge's conduct was visibly and audibly apparent to multiple individuals present. As I was exiting, I observed and heard crying and visible distress among those in attendance.

Other officers and individuals in the courtroom appeared visibly shocked and appalled by the misconduct.

After exiting the courtroom, multiple court staff members followed me out, apologizing for what I experienced and describing the judge's behavior as "disgusting."

The Victim's Assistance Police Officer who came to support me stated that he had never witnessed anything like it in his career as a Police Officer.

The District Attorney also apologized to me and informed the judge that her comments and tone were deeply inappropriate and harmful.

Impact on the Victim

The cumulative effect of these statements and behaviors caused profound emotional turmoil and grave psychological harm. It was deeply degrading, devastating and tormenting; and introduced thoughts of self-harm that I had not experienced in connection with these proceedings prior to that moment. These thoughts and feelings arose directly as a result of the Judge's statements, tone, and repeated minimization of the rape, now forming a permanent layer of trauma, in addition to the crime committed by the defendant.

Directly following the sentencing hearing, a Peer Crisis Responder from the CARES unit who was present expressed concern for my safety and emotional well-being based on the conduct he witnessed in the courtroom. Due to this concern, the responder ensured that I and my family were escorted safely, leaving the courthouse before the defendant's family, and personally drove us home to guarantee our safety. This intervention further reflects the severity of the psychological impact of the proceeding and the immediate safety concerns that arose as a result.

With conduct that aligns with systemic harm, institutional betrayal, and judicial/institutional retraumatization, the Judge's statements have created a source of psychological injury that now requires psychiatric intervention and ongoing recovery, and that I am forced to carry for the rest of my life.

Closing Statement

I am submitting this grievance not only for myself, but out of concern that no other victim should experience such exacerbation of their trauma; or be subjected to such dangerous rhetoric and precedents established during this sentencing proceeding. I submit this grievance to highlight the harm this poses to not only survivors but the community and justice system as a whole. Lastly, I also submit this grievance to request a formal review and corrective measures to protect and prevent similar harm to future survivors.

The conduct in my case is consistent with previous concerns raised by the Philadelphia legal community; including the District Attorney's Office, underscoring its broader impact on victims and public confidence in the judicial process.

I am not challenging the jury's verdict but rather reporting the manner in which the proceeding was conducted and how it affected my sense of safety, dignity, and justice. I remain deeply concerned for the safety, dignity, and well-being of survivors who will be subjected to similar treatment —particularly those who may not be physically or psychologically able to survive such conduct.

Thank you for taking the time to review my grievance; I sincerely appreciate your consideration and attention to this matter.

Respectfully Submitted,

Tiara Ileisha Singleton

ADDENDUM
To
Grievance

Addendum to Grievance Submitted To The Judicial Conduct Board of Pennsylvania

Re: Addendum to Grievance Regarding the Judge

From: Tiara Ileisha Singleton

Date: February 12, 2026

Dear Board Members,

This addendum supplements my original grievance, accepted on February 3, 2026, to provide updated information regarding developments since the sentencing hearing. It addresses issues related to victim participation, court scheduling, and the resulting professional, logistical, and psychological impacts that have occurred following the initial grievance submission.

Thank you for your careful attention and consideration.

Respectfully Submitted,

Tiara Ileisha Singleton

Body of Addendum

Re: Grievance Addendum — Victim Participation and Court Scheduling

Since submitting my grievance concerning the Judge, additional issues have arisen that directly implicate victim participation, procedural fairness, and the court's obligations under victim-rights protections.

1. Scheduling Conflicts and Impact on Victim Participation

Following the sentencing hearing, motions to reconsider sentence were filed by both the Commonwealth and defense counsel. A hearing on these motions (in the Judge's Court) was subsequently scheduled on a date that directly conflicted with a previously scheduled PSVI court proceeding (1501 Arch Street, Philadelphia, PA 19102) involving the same defendant and arising from the same underlying sexual violence case (Exhibit B & D).

The PSVI matter concerns a sexual violence restraining order essential to my safety and ongoing protection. That proceeding had been scheduled for February 6, 2026, since November 6, 2025, and was fixed and known to all parties for several months (Exhibit B). Both the defendant and I were required to appear.

Upon learning of this double booking (on January 23), I clearly communicated the scheduling conflict (for February 6) to the

District Attorney, requesting accommodations and inclusion in the process. As the victim in a sexual assault conviction, I have a recognized and substantial interest in proceedings that may alter the sentence imposed, particularly in light of the cumulative harm already detailed in my *grievance*.

On February 4, I was notified that the motion for reconsideration had been rescheduled from February 6, 2026 to February 9, 2026. In addition to taking time off from work to attend the (February 6) PSVI proceeding, I also took additional time off to appear on February 9 in the Judge's Court.

On February 9, I remained in the courthouse until approximately 1:00 p.m., at which time I was informed that the matter would not proceed and was instead postponed to February 13, 2026. Several explanations were offered for the delay, including the Judge proceeding with another trial in place of this scheduled motion, followed by defense counsel's departure.

Furthermore, on February 12, 2026 (at approximately 4:30 p.m.), after I had already taken additional time off from work and complied with all prior court requirements, I was notified by the District Attorney that the Judge canceled the motion for reconsideration entirely. I was also notified that her decision is for the defendant's sentence to remain unchanged.

These repeated delays and last-minute postponements required me to take additional time off from work on multiple occasions, often with little notice. As a result, my employer has required formal documentation to justify the pattern of absences in order to maintain my employment (Exhibit C). These employment consequences arise solely from court scheduling decisions outside of my control and underscore how unpredictable scheduling discourages meaningful victim participation.

These cancellations, combined with the ongoing accommodations for the defendant's employment, further demonstrate persistent preferential treatment afforded to the defendant and the resulting professional, constitutional, and logistical burdens imposed on me as the victim.

2. Preferential Treatment of Defendant and Judicial Conduct

By contrast, the defendant has received exceptions and accommodations for "work" despite being under house arrest and a convicted perpetrator. His house arrest conditions were modified to allow him to continue employment despite documented harassment I was facing from him and his family.

According to the full sentencing transcript (Exhibit A):

- The Judge instructed the defendant and his family to monitor my personal writings and online activity (pg36-37).
- She provided private access to her courtroom booth for conversation with the defendant, later involving his family(pg37).
- She waived all "supervision fees, costs, and fines" on his behalf (pg 30).
- She explicitly encouraged and endorsed the defendant and his family to "keep notes" and "keep track of everything" I posted, for his protection (pg 36-37). Further advising them to report to his attorney if necessary. This directive effectively places me in ongoing danger by authorizing the defendant and his family to surveil my personal expressions (**including potential locations of book signings,**

open mics and business events I post publicly), compromising my safety while already being a victim of his criminal conduct. Given the events personally witnessed, including instances where my mother had to intervene for my safety, she (my mother) has expressed serious concern for my well-being. This concern is further compounded by the cumulative events documented in these transcripts, the repeated delays and disruptions in court proceedings, and the fact that my prior police reports and the defendant's violations of the protection order have gone ignored.

- The defendant was permitted to request protection from me regarding my poetry, book content, and other personal works documenting how his criminal conduct altered my life (pg 36).

- The defendant also stated he was seeking protection against me for alleged contact and harassment, claiming he was "still getting things from her about this situation" (pg 36). These claims lacked any credibility or evidence. Notably, the defendant himself actually **ripped up the restraining order served to him while in court and destroyed the affidavit of service,** demonstrating disregard for the protections in place. Nevertheless, the Judge's Court encouraged and endorsed his request, authorizing ongoing surveillance without requiring proof.

- **Additional context not captured in the transcript: These actions and accusations occurred while I was not present in the courtroom.** The judge's laughter and dismissive tone during the proceedings obstructed my ability to safely and meaningfully participate in matters affecting my rights as a victim, and these circumstances were also not reflected in the transcript.

My absence was not incidental; it was a direct result of the judge's misconduct and created an environment in which I could not fully participate safely and effectively. The judge's laughing demeanor, along with the Court's facilitation and judicial endorsement of defendant monitoring, combined with repeated last-minute scheduling disruptions, compounded my professional, logistical, constitutional, and emotional burdens, creating an environment in which I could not fully participate within my constitutional rights to do so.

---

3. Impact and Need for Review

These disparities highlight an imbalance in how burdens are allocated — placing increasing logistical, professional, and psychological strain on the victim while affording flexibility to the defendant.

The repeated disruption of my ability to participate meaningfully in proceedings, coupled with judicial endorsement of defendant surveillance of my personal expressions, creates a dangerous precedent and warrants careful review to ensure judicial conduct reflects impartiality, fairness, safety, and respect for victim rights.

I respectfully request that the Board review these matters and take appropriate action to uphold victim rights, safety, and judicial integrity.

Thank you for your attention to these concerns and for your review of this matter.

Respectfully Submitted,

Tiara Ileisha Singleton

Public Court Docket

Philadelphia County
Court of Common Pleas, Pennsylvania
Case No. CP-51-CR-0007801-2023
Commonwealth of Pennsylvania
v.
Nafeece T. Beeks

Docket Entries:
October 20, 2023 – February 19, 2026
Official Public Record[1]

[1] All entries reproduced from the Official Court Docket via the Pennsylvania Unified Judicial System. Names and identifying details in the grievance section have been replaced with neutral titles for privacy and safety.

COURT OF COMMON PLEAS OF PHILADELPHIA COUNTY

DOCKET

Docket Number: CP-51-CR-0007801-2023

CRIMINAL DOCKET

Court Case

Commonwealth of Pennsylvania
v.
Nafeece T. Beeks

CASE INFORMATION

Judge Assigned: Brandeis-Roman, Tracy	Date Filed: 11/09/2023 Initiation Date: 11/09/2023
OTN: U 289942-2 LOTN:	Originating Docket No: MC-51-CR-0019008-2023
Initial Issuing Authority: Karen Y. Simmons	Final Issuing Authority:
Arresting Agency: Philadelphia Pd	Arresting Officer: Organ, Kimberly K.
Complaint/Citation No.: 2326033660-0019008	Incident Number: 2326033660
County: Philadelphia	Township: Philadelphia City

Case Local Number Type(s)	Case Local Number(s)
Originating Docket Number	MC-51-CR-0019008-2023
District Control Number	2326033660
Originating Document Number	2326033660-0019008

STATUS INFORMATION

Case Status: Closed

Arrest Date: 10/20/2023

Status Date	Processing Status
01/21/2026	Awaiting Post Sentence Motion Hearing Disposition
01/16/2026	Sentenced/Penalty Imposed
11/14/2025	Awaiting PSI
11/14/2025	Awaiting Sentencing
09/16/2025	Completed
08/08/2025	Awaiting PSI
08/08/2025	Awaiting Sentencing
08/08/2025	Awaiting Sentencing
04/21/2025	Awaiting Pre-Trial Conference
12/02/2024	Awaiting Pre-Trial Conference
06/10/2024	Awaiting Pre-Trial Conference
01/03/2024	Awaiting Trial
12/29/2023	Awaiting Pre-Trial Conference
12/12/2023	Awaiting Scheduling Conference
11/22/2023	Awaiting Pre-Trial Conference
11/09/2023	Awaiting Filing of Information

Complaint Date: 10/21/2023

COURT OF COMMON PLEAS OF PHILADELPHIA COUNTY

DOCKET

Docket Number: CP-51-CR-0007801-2023

CRIMINAL DOCKET

Court Case

Commonwealth of Pennsylvania
v.
Nafeece T. Beeks

CALENDAR EVENTS

Case Calendar Event Type	Schedule Start Date	Start Time	Room	Judge Name	Schedule Status
Formal Arraignment	11/22/2023	11:00 am	1104	Trial Commissioner Cynthia S. Gregg	Scheduled
Pre-Trial Conference	12/12/2023	9:00 am	905	Judge Zachary C. Shaffer	Scheduled
Scheduling Conference	12/29/2023	9:00 am	908	Judge Tracy Brandeis-Roman	Scheduled
Status	01/03/2024	9:00 am	908	Judge Tracy Brandeis-Roman	Scheduled
Pre-Trial Conference	06/05/2024	9:00 am	908	Judge Tracy Brandeis-Roman	Scheduled
Jury Trial	06/10/2024	9:00 am	908	Judge Tracy Brandeis-Roman	Continued
Pre-Trial Conference	11/27/2024	9:00 am	908	Judge Tracy Brandeis-Roman	Scheduled
Jury Trial	12/02/2024	9:00 am	908	Judge Tracy Brandeis-Roman	Continued
Pre-Trial Conference	04/16/2025	9:00 am	908	Judge Tracy Brandeis-Roman	Scheduled
Jury Trial	04/21/2025	9:00 am	908	Judge Tracy Brandeis-Roman	Continued
Pre-Trial Conference	07/22/2025	9:00 am	908	Judge Tracy Brandeis-Roman	Scheduled
Pre-Trial Conference	07/25/2025	9:00 am	908	Judge Tracy Brandeis-Roman	Cancelled
Jury Trial	08/04/2025	9:00 am	908	Judge Tracy Brandeis-Roman	Continued
Jury Trial	08/05/2025	9:00 am	908	Judge Tracy Brandeis-Roman	Continued
Jury Trial	08/06/2025	9:00 am	908	Judge Tracy Brandeis-Roman	Continued
Jury Trial	08/07/2025	9:00 am	908	Judge Tracy Brandeis-Roman	Continued
Jury Trial	08/08/2025	9:00 am	908	Judge Tracy Brandeis-Roman	Scheduled
Surrender	08/26/2025	9:00 am	908	Judge Tracy Brandeis-Roman	Scheduled
Surrender	09/16/2025	9:00 am	908	Judge Tracy Brandeis-Roman	Scheduled
Sentencing	11/14/2025	9:00 am	908	Judge Tracy Brandeis-Roman	Continued
Sentencing	01/16/2026	9:00 am	908	Judge Tracy Brandeis-Roman	Scheduled
Reconsideration Hearing	02/09/2026	9:00 am	908	Judge Tracy Brandeis-Roman	Continued
Reconsideration Hearing	02/13/2026	9:00 am	908	Judge Tracy Brandeis-Roman	Cancelled

CONFINEMENT INFORMATION

Confinement Known As Of	Confinement Type	Destination Location	Confinement Reason	Still in Custody
01/16/2026	County Correctional Facility	Phila Industrial Corr Center		Yes

COURT OF COMMON PLEAS OF PHILADELPHIA COUNTY

DOCKET

Docket Number: CP-51-CR-0007801-2023

CRIMINAL DOCKET

Court Case

Commonwealth of Pennsylvania
v.
Nafeece T. Beeks

DEFENDANT INFORMATION

Date Of Birth: 11/28/1994 City/State/Zip: PHILADELPHIA, PA 19122

CASE PARTICIPANTS

Participant Type	Name
Defendant	Beeks, Nafeece T.

BAIL INFORMATION

Beeks, Nafeece T. **Nebbia Status: None**

Bail Action	Date	Bail Type	Originating Court	Percentage	Amount
Set	10/21/2023	Monetary	Municipal Court	10.00%	$500,000.00
Decrease Bail Amount	10/27/2023	Monetary	Municipal Court	10.00%	$100,000.00
Set (bail modification)	10/27/2023	Monetary	Municipal Court		$100,000.00

Surety Type	Surety Name	Posting Status	Posting Date	Security Type	Security Amt
Third Party	ABC Bail Bonds	Posted	10/27/2023	Surety Bonds	$100,000.00

CHARGES

Seq.	Orig Seq.	Grade	Statute	Statute Description	Offense Dt.	OTN
1	1	F1	**18 § 3121 §§ A1**	Rape Forcible Compulsion	08/05/2023	U 289942-2
2	2	F1	**18 § 3123 §§ A1**	IDSI Forcible Compulsion	08/05/2023	U 289942-2
3	3	F2	**18 § 2902 §§ A1**	Unlawful Restraint/ Serious Bodily Injury	08/05/2023	U 289942-2
4	4	F2	**18 § 3124.1**	Sexual Assault	08/05/2023	U 289942-2
5	5	M1	**18 § 3126 §§ A2**	Indecent Assault Forcible Compulsion	08/05/2023	U 289942-2
6	6	M2	**18 § 3126 §§ A1**	Indec Asslt-W/O Cons Of Other	08/05/2023	U 289942-2
7	7	M2	**18 § 3127 §§ A**	Indecent Exposure	08/05/2023	U 289942-2
8	8	F2	**18 § 3125 §§ A2**	Agg. Ind. Assault - Forcible Compulsion	08/05/2023	U 289942-2

DISPOSITION SENTENCING/PENALTIES

Disposition
Case Event — Disposition Date — Final Disposition
Sequence/Description — Offense Disposition — Grade — Section
Sentencing Judge — Sentence Date — Credit For Time Served
Sentence/Diversion Program Type — Incarceration/Diversionary Period — Start Date
Sentence Conditions

Lower Court Proceeding (generic)

Case Event / Sequence/Description	Disposition Date / Offense Disposition	Final Disposition / Grade	Section
Preliminary Hearing	11/08/2023	Not Final	
1 / Rape Forcible Compulsion	Held for Court	F1	18 § 3121 §§ A1
2 / IDSI Forcible Compulsion	Held for Court	F1	18 § 3123 §§ A1
3 / Unlawful Restraint/ Serious Bodily Injury	Held for Court	F2	18 § 2902 §§ A1
4 / Sexual Assault	Held for Court	F2	18 § 3124.1
5 / Indecent Assault Forcible Compulsion	Held for Court	M1	18 § 3126 §§ A2

DISPOSITION SENTENCING/PENALTIES

Disposition Case Event Sequence/Description Sentencing Judge Sentence/Diversion Program Type Sentence Conditions	Disposition Date Offense Disposition Sentence Date Incarceration/Diversionary Period	Final Disposition Grade	Section Credit For Time Served Start Date
6 / Indec Asslt-W/O Cons Of Other	Held for Court	M2	18 § 3126 §§ A1
7 / Indecent Exposure	Held for Court	M2	18 § 3127 §§ A
8 / Agg. Ind. Assault - Forcible Compulsion	Held for Court	F2	18 § 3125 §§ A2
Proceed to Court Defendant Was Not Present			
Information Filed	11/14/2023	Not Final	
1 / Rape Forcible Compulsion	Proceed to Court	F1	18 § 3121 §§ A1
2 / IDSI Forcible Compulsion	Proceed to Court	F1	18 § 3123 §§ A1
3 / Unlawful Restraint/ Serious Bodily Injury	Proceed to Court	F2	18 § 2902 §§ A1
4 / Sexual Assault	Proceed to Court	F2	18 § 3124.1
5 / Indecent Assault Forcible Compulsion	Proceed to Court	M1	18 § 3126 §§ A2
6 / Indec Asslt-W/O Cons Of Other	Proceed to Court	M2	18 § 3126 §§ A1
7 / Indecent Exposure	Proceed to Court	M2	18 § 3127 §§ A
8 / Agg. Ind. Assault - Forcible Compulsion	Proceed to Court	F2	18 § 3125 §§ A2
Guilty			
Jury Trial	08/08/2025	Final Disposition	
1 / Rape Forcible Compulsion	Guilty	F1	18 § 3121 §§ A1
Brandeis-Roman, Tracy	01/16/2026		
Confinement	Min of 11.00 Months 15.00 Days Max of 23.00 Months 11 1/2 - 23 months		01/16/2026
Court Costs Waived Credit to be calculated by the Phila. Prison System To stay away from victim. Must register with the State Police and comply with all Tier III Megan's Law requirements. No parole at minimum.			
Probation	Max of 3.00 Years 3 years		
2 / IDSI Forcible Compulsion	Not Guilty	F1	18 § 3123 §§ A1
Brandeis-Roman, Tracy	01/16/2026		
3 / Unlawful Restraint/ Serious Bodily Injury	Nolle Prossed	F2	18 § 2902 §§ A1
Brandeis-Roman, Tracy	01/16/2026		
4 / Sexual Assault	Not Guilty	F2	18 § 3124.1
Brandeis-Roman, Tracy	01/16/2026		

COURT OF COMMON PLEAS OF PHILADELPHIA COUNTY

DOCKET

Docket Number: CP-51-CR-0007801-2023

CRIMINAL DOCKET

Court Case

Commonwealth of Pennsylvania
v.
Nafeece T. Beeks

DISPOSITION SENTENCING/PENALTIES

Disposition / Case Event / Sequence/Description / Sentencing Judge / Sentence/Diversion Program Type / Sentence Conditions	Disposition Date / Offense Disposition / Sentence Date / Incarceration/Diversionary Period	Final Disposition / Grade	Section / Credit For Time Served / Start Date
5 / Indecent Assault Forcible Compulsion	Nolle Prossed	M1	18 § 3126 §§ A2
Brandeis-Roman, Tracy	01/16/2026		
6 / Indec Asslt-W/O Cons Of Other	Nolle Prossed	M2	18 § 3126 §§ A1
Brandeis-Roman, Tracy	01/16/2026		
7 / Indecent Exposure	Nolle Prossed	M2	18 § 3127 §§ A
Brandeis-Roman, Tracy	01/16/2026		
8 / Agg. Ind. Assault - Forcible Compulsion	Nolle Prossed	F2	18 § 3125 §§ A2
Brandeis-Roman, Tracy	01/16/2026		

LINKED SENTENCES:

Link 1

CP-51-CR-0007801-2023 - Seq. No. 1 (18 § 3121 §§ A1) - Probation is Consecutive to
CP-51-CR-0007801-2023 - Seq. No. 1 (18 § 3121 §§ A1) - Confinement

COMMONWEALTH INFORMATION

Name:

Supreme Court No:

ATTORNEY INFORMATION

Name: Todd Michael Mosser
Private

Supreme Court No: 087534

Rep. Status: Active

Phone Number(s):

Address:

ENTRIES

Sequence Number	CP Filed Date	Document Date	Filed By
1	11/09/2023		Court of Common Pleas - Philadelphia County
Held for Court			
1	11/14/2023		Krasner, Larry
Information Filed			
3	11/22/2023		Court of Common Pleas - Philadelphia County
Hearing Notice			

ENTRIES

Sequence Number	CP Filed Date	Document Date	Filed By
4 Hearing Notice	12/12/2023		Court of Common Pleas - Philadelphia County
5 Pre-Trial Conference Held	12/12/2023		Lightsey, Chesley
1 Scheduling Conference Held	12/29/2023		Brandeis-Roman, Tracy
4 Hearing Notice	12/29/2023		Court of Common Pleas - Philadelphia County
7 Hearing Notice	12/29/2023		Court of Common Pleas - Philadelphia County
10 Hearing Notice	12/29/2023		Court of Common Pleas - Philadelphia County
1 Order Granting Motion to Modify House Arrest	01/03/2024		Brandeis-Roman, Tracy
2 Order Granting Motion to Modify House Arrest	01/03/2024		Brandeis-Roman, Tracy
3 Trial Date to Remain	01/03/2024		Brandeis-Roman, Tracy
1 Hearing Notice	06/05/2024		Court of Common Pleas - Philadelphia County
4 Hearing Notice	06/10/2024		Court of Common Pleas - Philadelphia County

COURT OF COMMON PLEAS OF PHILADELPHIA COUNTY

DOCKET

Docket Number: CP-51-CR-0007801-2023

CRIMINAL DOCKET

Court Case

Commonwealth of Pennsylvania
v.
Nafeece T. Beeks

ENTRIES

Sequence Number	CP Filed Date	Document Date	Filed By
5	06/10/2024		Court of Common Pleas - Philadelphia County
Hearing Notice			
6	06/10/2024		Brandeis-Roman, Tracy
Defense Advance Request For Continuance			
9	06/10/2024		Court of Common Pleas - Philadelphia County
Hearing Notice			
10	06/10/2024		Brandeis-Roman, Tracy
Order Granting Motion to Modify House Arrest			
1	11/27/2024		Brandeis-Roman, Tracy
Pre-Trial Conference Held			
2	11/27/2024		Court of Common Pleas - Philadelphia County
Short Certificate Pretrial Electronic Monitoring 11/27/2024			
4	12/02/2024		Court of Common Pleas - Philadelphia County
Hearing Notice			
5	12/02/2024		Court of Common Pleas - Philadelphia County
Hearing Notice			
8	12/02/2024		Court of Common Pleas - Philadelphia County
Hearing Notice			
9	12/02/2024		Brandeis-Roman, Tracy
Defense Advance Request For Continuance			
1	04/16/2025		Brandeis-Roman, Tracy
Pre-Trial Conference Held			

ENTRIES

Sequence Number	CP Filed Date	Document Date	Filed By
4	04/21/2025		Court of Common Pleas - Philadelphia County
Hearing Notice			
6	04/21/2025		Court of Common Pleas - Philadelphia County
Hearing Notice			
8	04/21/2025		Court of Common Pleas - Philadelphia County
Hearing Notice			
9	04/21/2025		Brandeis-Roman, Tracy
Defense Request For Continuance For Further Investigation			
3	07/17/2025		Court of Common Pleas - Philadelphia County
Hearing Notice			
1	07/22/2025		Brandeis-Roman, Tracy
Pre-Trial Conference Held			
4	08/04/2025		Brandeis-Roman, Tracy
Defense Request For Continuance Attorney Unavailable			
4	08/05/2025		Court of Common Pleas - Philadelphia County
Hearing Notice			
5	08/05/2025		Brandeis-Roman, Tracy
Jury Selection Continued			
4	08/06/2025		Court of Common Pleas - Philadelphia County
Hearing Notice			
5	08/06/2025		Brandeis-Roman, Tracy
Jury Selection Completed			
6	08/06/2025		Brandeis-Roman, Tracy
Defendant Arraigned and Notice of Rights and Procedures Explained			

COURT OF COMMON PLEAS OF PHILADELPHIA COUNTY

DOCKET

Docket Number: CP-51-CR-0007801-2023

CRIMINAL DOCKET

Court Case

Commonwealth of Pennsylvania
v.
Nafeece T. Beeks

ENTRIES

Sequence Number	CP Filed Date	Document Date	Filed By
7 Testimony Begins	08/06/2025		Brandeis-Roman, Tracy
4 Hearing Notice	08/07/2025		Court of Common Pleas - Philadelphia County
5 Closing Arguments	08/07/2025		Brandeis-Roman, Tracy
6 Testimony Concludes	08/07/2025		Brandeis-Roman, Tracy
1 Question from Juror	08/08/2025		Brandeis-Roman, Tracy
2 Guilty	08/08/2025		Brandeis-Roman, Tracy
3 Order Entering an Exhibit	08/08/2025		Brandeis-Roman, Tracy
6 Hearing Notice	08/08/2025		Court of Common Pleas - Philadelphia County
8 Hearing Notice	08/08/2025		Court of Common Pleas - Philadelphia County
9 Order -- Trial Disposition	08/08/2025		Court of Common Pleas - Philadelphia County
10 Short Certificate	08/08/2025		Court of Common Pleas - Philadelphia County

COURT OF COMMON PLEAS OF PHILADELPHIA COUNTY

DOCKET

Docket Number: CP-51-CR-0007801-2023

CRIMINAL DOCKET

Court Case

Commonwealth of Pennsylvania
v.
Nafeece T. Beeks

ENTRIES

Sequence Number	CP Filed Date	Document Date	Filed By
11	08/08/2025		Court of Common Pleas - Philadelphia County
Short Certificate			
2	08/26/2025		Court of Common Pleas - Philadelphia County
Hearing Notice			
3	08/26/2025		Brandeis-Roman, Tracy
Order Granting Motion for Continuance			
1	09/16/2025		Brandeis-Roman, Tracy
Defendant Surrendered			
4	11/14/2025		Court of Common Pleas - Philadelphia County
Hearing Notice			
5	11/14/2025		Brandeis-Roman, Tracy
Sentence Further Deferred Defense Request			
1	01/16/2026		Brandeis-Roman, Tracy
Order - Sentence/Penalty Imposed			
3	01/16/2026		Court of Common Pleas - Philadelphia County
Court Commitment State or County Correctional Institution Philadelphia Department of Prisons 01/16/2026			
4	01/16/2026		Court of Common Pleas - Philadelphia County
Short Certificate Philadelphia Department of Prisons 01/16/2026			
5	01/16/2026		Brandeis-Roman, Tracy
Order Entering an Exhibit			
1	01/21/2026		Abdul-Rahman, Qawi
Motion for Reconsideration of Sentence			

COURT OF COMMON PLEAS OF PHILADELPHIA COUNTY

DOCKET

Docket Number: CP-51-CR-0007801-2023

CRIMINAL DOCKET

Court Case

Commonwealth of Pennsylvania
v.
Nafeece T. Beeks

ENTRIES

Sequence Number	CP Filed Date	Document Date	Filed By
1	01/22/2026		Philadelphia County District Attorney's Office
Motion for Modification of Sentence			
2	01/23/2026		Court of Common Pleas - Philadelphia County
Hearing Notice			
3	02/03/2026		Court of Common Pleas - Philadelphia County
Hearing Notice			
1	02/05/2026		Mosser, Todd Michael
Entry of Appearance			
4	02/09/2026		Court of Common Pleas - Philadelphia County
Hearing Notice			
5	02/09/2026		Brandeis-Roman, Tracy
Court Request For Continuance Court is on Trial			
2	02/12/2026		Brandeis-Roman, Tracy
Order Denying Motion for Reconsideration			
1	02/17/2026		Philadelphia County District Attorney's Office
Supplemental Post Sentence Motion			
1	02/19/2026		Brandeis-Roman, Tracy
Order Vacating Denial of CW Motion for Reconsideration of Sentence			
2	02/19/2026		Brandeis-Roman, Tracy
Order Granting CW Motion for Leave to File Supplemental Post Sentence Motion			

Docket Number: CP-51-CR-0007801-2023

CRIMINAL DOCKET

Court Case

Commonwealth of Pennsylvania
v.
Nafeece T. Beeks

CASE FINANCIAL INFORMATION

Last Payment Date: 01/21/2026 — Total of Last Payment: -$12.50

Beeks, Nafeece T. Defendant	Assessment	Payments	Adjustments	Non Monetary Payments	Balance
Costs/Fees					
Motion Filing Fee (Philadelphia)	$12.50	$0.00	($12.50)	$0.00	$0.00
Bail Bond (Philadelphia)	$10.00	$0.00	($10.00)	$0.00	$0.00
Motion Filing Fee (Philadelphia)	$12.50	($12.50)	$0.00	$0.00	$0.00
Costs/Fees Totals:	$35.00	($12.50)	($22.50)	$0.00	$0.00
Grand Totals:	$35.00	($12.50)	($22.50)	$0.00	$0.00

** - Indicates assessment is subrogated

www.ingramcontent.com/pod-product-compliance
Lightning Source LLC
LaVergne TN
LVHW090336210926
848480LV00004B/1434